Heroine Addict

"Journaling your way to becoming addicted to the heroine you are."

"God is in the midst of her, she will not be moved; God will help her when morning dawns." - Psalm 46:5

This journal, although filled with scriptures and biblical references, it is simply the thoughts of the author. It is not intended to answer every question you may be wrestling with but the author hopes it pushes you to believe in yourself.

"God is in the midst of her, she will not be moved; God will help her when morning dawns." - Psalm 46:5

Dedication

To the woman who has to face each day pulling strength from places you didn't know existed and crying tears from areas that should have long dried up. Yet, you work a little harder, give a little more and smile while often being overlooked, overused and underpaid.

This journal is dedicated to you.

Thank you for never giving up, even when it seems like the easiest thing to do.

———————————

I must also dedicate this to the young lady who pushed me to finish this journal, Ms. TJ Jefferson. May the work of your hands and the brilliance of your mind never run out. You are the epitome of a HEROINE!

"God is in the midst of her, she will not be moved; God will help her when morning dawns." - Psalm 46:5

My Thanks

As always, I have to thank God for entrusting me with such an amazing gift. Every time I write, I am even more grateful to Him for choosing a girl who looks like me, the one society counted out, long ago, to carry a mantle some say I never would. Thank you God for the chance to prove them wrong and you right.

And to every person who encourages me, daily. My family, friends, social media and blog followers and to each of you who share my thoughts and posts. Most importantly, to those of you who pray for me. THANK YOU!

And to Angel Bearfield who always creates the most amazing book covers. May God never allow your creativity to run out.

If I had more pages, I'd name all of you. If I had longer arms, I'd hug each of you. If I had more time ...

Instead, I'll simply say, THANK YOU!

"God is in the midst of her, she will not be moved; God will help her when morning dawns." - Psalm 46:5

Dear Heroine,

I often tell people, I'm just a mere brown girl whom God chooses to use. I don't work for accolades or to fit in because let me be honest. I'm a preacher who writes about sex, I still sometimes curse, I have tattoos and walk in 5 inch heels, confidently. I am whose I am.

Then one day, I was chosen as a Heroine Legacy Honoree by Tamika Jefferson and it blew my mind to know she thought enough of me.

Now, here you are. Whether you are reading this journal because you have been chosen as a Heroine Legacy Honoree or simply because you are ready to become addicted to the Heroine you are, know I believe in you.

From this day forward, walk boldly Heroine, with your head held high because God made you strong. Even if I don't personally know you, I believe you exemplify what a heroine is. And because you believe in yourself enough to open this book, I declare this is only the beginning of what God has in store for you.

Oh, just so you know, this journey is not and will not be easy but it is doggone sure worth it!

— Lakisha

"God is in the midst of her, she will not be moved; God will help her when morning dawns." - Psalm 46:5

You are probably asking, why is this journal different from all the rest? After all, it is another book filled with blank pages intended for your thoughts, affirmations, poems, scriptures and etc.; however, this journal was created in the hope you will become addicted to heroine.

No, not the drug but the woman you are and destined to become. The woman who is admired by others, who is held in high regard, who is favorable and filled with courage. The woman who is honorable and of good quality.

This journal was created, through prayer, in order to encourage you to search for, find, pull out and then display the heroine within you because your destiny depends on her surviving.

"God is in the midst of her, she will not be moved; God will help her when morning dawns." - Psalm 46:5

A few questions ...

1. Are you ready to be a Heroine Addict who is so addicted that you stop taking you, your dreams and your destiny for granted?

2. Are you ready to be a Heroine Addict who is so addicted that you don't care who knows so you walk with your head held high, owning it?

3. Are you ready to be a Heroine Addict who is so addicted that you stop listening to the naysayers and instead proudly proclaim, "I'm a Heroine ADDICT, addicted to the greatness within me?"

"God is in the midst of her, she will not be moved; God will help her when morning dawns." - Psalm 46:5

And blessed is she that believed: for there shall be a performance of those things which were told her from the Lord.

– Luke 1:45

"God is in the midst of her, she will not be moved; God will help her when morning dawns." - Psalm 46:5

How can I become a Heroine Addict?

By symbolizing what a heroine is.

We do this by breaking down the letters of HEROINE into single words we, by the guidance of the Holy Spirit, hope will help you become the best you God intended.

This journal is not intended to overload you with words, scriptures or prayers, neither is it set to specific days or times. We don't have a plan attached because we want you to take as much time as you need to step into your rightful place, journaling your thoughts after each section until you are confident enough to move to the next word.

So grab a pen and your bible and let's get you addicted to the HEROINE you are!

"God is in the midst of her, she will not be moved; God will help her when morning dawns." - Psalm 46:5

"For we are his workmanship, created in Christ Jesus for good works, which God prepared beforehand, that we should walk in them."

Ephesians 2:10

"God is in the midst of her, she will not be moved; God will help her when morning dawns." - Psalm 46:5

Her·o·ine

ˈherōən/

Noun

A woman admired or idealized for her courage, outstanding achievements, or noble qualities.

"Who can find a virtuous woman? For her price is far above rubies."

Proverbs 31:10

"God is in the midst of her, she will not be moved; God will help her when morning dawns." - Psalm 46:5

HEROINE

abitable

hab·it·a·ble

/ˈhabədəb(ə)l/

adjective

> *Suitable or good enough to live in.*

When you are preparing to buy a home, an inspection is ordered by the company who will finance your loan. It is the inspector's responsibility to ensure the dwelling is fit enough to live in by making sure the foundation is solid, the walls are capable of withstanding a storm and there are no mistakes that can be costly to the one making the purchase. The inspection is also to gage the worth of the dwelling.

In other words, it needs to be habitable.

As children of God, our dwelling (body) needs to be habitable to the Holy Spirit. Bible shares in Romans 8:9, "You, however, are not in the flesh but in the Spirit, if in fact the Spirit of God dwells in you.

"God is in the midst of her, she will not be moved; God will help her when morning dawns." - Psalm 46:5

Anyone who does not have the Spirit of Christ does not belong to him."

When the Spirit lives within us, He is then able to intercede on our behalf when we are being imposed upon by the enemy. When we are habitable and the Spirit is within us, He strengthens us to handle the storm of situations and withstand the winds of warfare. When the Spirit is in us, we can handle the hardships of hurt, strains of sickness and the affliction of abuse.

This leads me to ask you the question ... are you habitable? Are you fit enough to live in? Is your dwelling safe enough to survive going through a storm or will it crumble at the first sign of high winds? Are you worth the value attached to your being?

Dear God,

Make me habitable. Inspect me and remove anything or anyone that may cause me to fail your inspection. Search me for I am willing and ready to be made over. Clean me up and make me suitable for your service and worthy of my value.

Amen.

_____

_____

_____

_____

_____

_____

_____

_____

_____

_____

_____

_____

_____

_____

"God is in the midst of her, she will not be moved; God will help her when morning dawns." - Psalm 46:5

_____

_____

_____

_____

_____

_____

_____

_____

_____

_____

_____

_____

_____

_____

"God is in the midst of her, she will not be moved; God will help her when morning dawns." - Psalm 46:5

_____

_____

_____

_____

_____

_____

_____

_____

_____

_____

_____

_____

_____

_____

_____

_____

"God is in the midst of her, she will not be moved; God will help her when morning dawns." - Psalm 46:5

_____

_____

_____

_____

_____

_____

_____

_____

_____

_____

_____

_____

_____

_____

_____

"God is in the midst of her, she will not be moved; God will help her when morning dawns." - Psalm 46:5

_____

_____

_____

_____

_____

_____

_____

_____

_____

_____

_____

_____

_____

_____

"God is in the midst of her, she will not be moved; God will help her when morning dawns." - Psalm 46:5

_____

_____

_____

_____

_____

_____

_____

_____

_____

_____

_____

_____

_____

_____

"God is in the midst of her, she will not be moved; God will help her when morning dawns." - Psalm 46:5

_____

_____

_____

_____

_____

_____

_____

_____

_____

_____

_____

_____

_____

_____

_____

"God is in the midst of her, she will not be moved; God will help her when morning dawns." - Psalm 46:5

_____

_____

_____

_____

_____

_____

_____

_____

_____

_____

_____

_____

_____

"God is in the midst of her, she will not be moved; God will help her when morning dawns." - Psalm 46:5

_____

_____

_____

_____

_____

_____

_____

_____

_____

_____

_____

_____

_____

_____

"God is in the midst of her, she will not be moved; God will help her when morning dawns." - Psalm 46:5

hEROINE

"God is in the midst of her, she will not be moved; God will help her when morning dawns." - Psalm 46:5

mbody

em·bod·y

/ əmˈbädē/

verb

Be an expression of or give a tangible or visible form to.

When a woman gives birth and people see the baby, one of the first things said is, "he/she looks just like ..." As children of God, can it be said that you look like your father? No, I am not referring to the physical appearance but will I be able to tell you're a child of God by your actions?

In other words, do we embody the presence of God in our living, giving, talking and walking?

Understand, we are not made to look like God because no one has seen Him but we are created in the likeness of His spiritual attributes.

What are those attributes? Some are; love, forgiveness, kindness, holiness, wisdom, truth, grace, mercy, longsuffering and etc.

As a heroine, you should carry these traits making it easy for someone to recognize the spirit you embody. Sure, there will be days when the harshness of flesh rears its ugly head but those days should be less than the good days. After all, a Heroine should be known for her noble qualities, at all times and not when it is convenient.

Leading me to ask, what do you embody? Is your image that of wickedness or wisdom, holiness or hellish, love and kindness or hateful and mean? Because the bible shares in 1 Corinthians 15:49, "Just as we have borne the image of the man of dust, we shall also bear the image of the man of heaven."

Dear God,

Forgive me for the times I don't represent You well. Forgive me for the times I take You for granted. I know I am a representation of You and I will, from this point on, seek to make you proud. Amen.

"God is in the midst of her, she will not be moved; God will help her when morning dawns." - Psalm 46:5

_____

_____

_____

_____

_____

_____

_____

_____

_____

_____

_____

_____

_____

_____

_____

"God is in the midst of her, she will not be moved; God will help her when morning dawns." - Psalm 46:5

_____

_____

_____

_____

_____

_____

_____

_____

_____

_____

_____

_____

_____

_____

_____

_____

"God is in the midst of her, she will not be moved; God will help her when morning dawns." - Psalm 46:5

_____

_____

_____

_____

_____

_____

_____

_____

_____

_____

_____

_____

_____

_____

_____

"God is in the midst of her, she will not be moved; God will help her when morning dawns." - Psalm 46:5

_____

_____

_____

_____

_____

_____

_____

_____

_____

_____

_____

_____

_____

"God is in the midst of her, she will not be moved; God will help her when morning dawns." - Psalm 46:5

_____

_____

_____

_____

_____

_____

_____

_____

_____

_____

_____

_____

_____

_____

"God is in the midst of her, she will not be moved; God will help her when morning dawns." - Psalm 46:5

_____

_____

_____

_____

_____

_____

_____

_____

_____

_____

_____

_____

_____

_____

"God is in the midst of her, she will not be moved; God will help her when morning dawns." - Psalm 46:5

_____

_____

_____

_____

_____

_____

_____

_____

_____

_____

_____

_____

_____

_____

"God is in the midst of her, she will not be moved; God will help her when morning dawns." - Psalm 46:5

_____

_____

_____

_____

_____

_____

_____

_____

_____

_____

_____

_____

_____

_____

"God is in the midst of her, she will not be moved; God will help her when morning dawns." - Psalm 46:5

_____

_____

_____

_____

_____

_____

_____

_____

_____

_____

_____

_____

_____

_____

"God is in the midst of her, she will not be moved; God will help her when morning dawns." - Psalm 46:5

HE**R**OINE

efine

re·fine

/ rə'fīn/

verb

Remove impurities or unwanted elements from a substance.

Do you wonder, as I sometimes do, why God even bothers with us? We lie, cheat, steal, kill, rob, defame, abuse, sin and more importantly, we sometimes mistreat God yet He still shows up.

Not only that but He still provides, He still heals, He still glorifies, He still sanctifies and He still protects. Yet, I have come to understand, God doesn't do what He does because of us, He does it because it is His reputation on the line.

For we are His namesake, made in His likeness and because of this, we have to be habitable and then embody His spirit. However, in order to do this, God has to sometimes take us through the fire; not to kill us but to refine us.

"God is in the midst of her, she will not be moved; God will help her when morning dawns." - Psalm 46:5

The bible shares in Malachi 3:1-3, "Behold, I send my messenger, and he will prepare the way before me. And the Lord whom you seek will suddenly come to his temple; and the messenger of the covenant in whom you delight, behold, he is coming, says the LORD of hosts. But who can endure the day of his coming, and who can stand when he appears? For he is like a refiner's fire and like fullers' soap. He will sit as a refiner and purifier of silver, and he will purify the sons of Levi and refine them like gold and silver, and they will bring offerings in righteousness to the LORD."

You see, in order for us to boldly stand as the heroines we are, we have to be refined because it is in this process the impurities, which have attached themselves to us, are removed. So, those days when it feels like the fire is getting hotter and you have more chaos than calm; this is God refining us.

"For my own name's sake I delay my wrath; for the sake of my praise I hold it back from you, so as not to destroy you completely. See, I have refined you, though not as silver; I have tested you in the furnace of affliction. For my own sake, for my own sake, I do this. How can I let myself be defamed? I will not yield my glory to another." – Isaiah 48:9-11

Dear God,

Thank you for my period of refinement because I now know it's to purify me. Give me the strength to stand and the courage to endure until you turn down the fire and I come out shining as pure gold.

Amen.

"God is in the midst of her, she will not be moved; God will help her when morning dawns." - Psalm 46:5

_____

_____

_____

_____

_____

_____

_____

_____

_____

_____

_____

_____

_____

_____

"God is in the midst of her, she will not be moved; God will help her when morning dawns." - Psalm 46:5

_____

_____

_____

_____

_____

_____

_____

_____

_____

_____

_____

_____

_____

_____

"God is in the midst of her, she will not be moved; God will help her when morning dawns." - Psalm 46:5

_____

_____

_____

_____

_____

_____

_____

_____

_____

_____

_____

_____

_____

_____

"God is in the midst of her, she will not be moved; God will help her when morning dawns." - Psalm 46:5

_____

_____

_____

_____

_____

_____

_____

_____

_____

_____

_____

_____

_____

_____

_____

_____

"God is in the midst of her, she will not be moved; God will help her when morning dawns." - Psalm 46:5

"God is in the midst of her, she will not be moved; God will help her when morning dawns." - Psalm 46:5

_____

_____

_____

_____

_____

_____

_____

_____

_____

_____

_____

_____

_____

_____

"God is in the midst of her, she will not be moved; God will help her when morning dawns." - Psalm 46:5

_____

_____

_____

_____

_____

_____

_____

_____

_____

_____

_____

_____

_____

_____

_____

"God is in the midst of her, she will not be moved; God will help her when morning dawns." - Psalm 46:5

_____

_____

_____

_____

_____

_____

_____

_____

_____

_____

_____

_____

_____

_____

_____

_____

"God is in the midst of her, she will not be moved; God will help her when morning dawns." - Psalm 46:5

_____

_____

_____

_____

_____

_____

_____

_____

_____

_____

_____

_____

_____

_____

_____

"God is in the midst of her, she will not be moved; God will help her when morning dawns." - Psalm 46:5

utward

out·ward

/ ˈoutwərd/

adjective

> *Of, on, or from the outside*

Once upon a time, there was a young lady who would eat alone because no one invited her to sit with them. At work functions, she was usually by herself and she couldn't understand why. She considered herself to be friendly but nobody dared to come up to her.

One day she got up the courage to ask the lady in the cubicle next to her, "Excuse me, why don't you ever talk to me?" The lady replies, "Because your face tells me to stay away."

Some people may read this and say, "I don't care what people think" but do you not care how you look? In Nehemiah 2:2, the king asked Nehemiah,

"God is in the midst of her, she will not be moved; God will help her when morning dawns." - Psalm 46:5

"Why is your face sad, seeing you are not sick? This is nothing but sadness of the heart."

What is your external reflecting? Is it showing your past mistakes or the miraculous work of the master? Is it showing the struggle or the fact you survived? Does your face hold fear or your willingness to fight?

Does your outward appearance show you are a child of God or will I have to ask you? Look, you are a HEROINE which means we celebrate you for your courage to push without counting the times you have fallen. We rejoice for your triumphs without keeping track of the times you were denied.

This is not about how you dress but it is everything about the way you carry yourself. Beloved, carry yourself like the victorious superwoman you are even if you just came out the battle and lost. Express yourself for who your destiny says you will become and not for what the natural tries to convince you to be.

Dear God,

I am wonderfully and fearfully made so I will act like it. You made me to be an heir to the kingdom so I will portray the royalty I am. Forgive me for the times my outer didn't match my destiny, I know better now. Thank you for giving me another chance to walk in the greatness that is you.

"God is in the midst of her, she will not be moved; God will help her when morning dawns." - Psalm 46:5

_____

_____

_____

_____

_____

_____

_____

_____

_____

_____

_____

_____

_____

_____

"God is in the midst of her, she will not be moved; God will help her when morning dawns." - Psalm 46:5

_____

_____

_____

_____

_____

_____

_____

_____

_____

_____

_____

_____

_____

_____

"God is in the midst of her, she will not be moved; God will help her when morning dawns." - Psalm 46:5

_____

_____

_____

_____

_____

_____

_____

_____

_____

_____

_____

_____

_____

_____

"God is in the midst of her, she will not be moved; God will help her when morning dawns." - Psalm 46:5

Journal to Destiny

_____

_____

_____

_____

_____

_____

_____

_____

_____

_____

_____

_____

_____

_____

"God is in the midst of her, she will not be moved; God will help her when morning dawns." - Psalm 46:5

_____

_____

_____

_____

_____

_____

_____

_____

_____

_____

_____

_____

_____

_____

"God is in the midst of her, she will not be moved; God will help her when morning dawns." - Psalm 46:5

_____

_____

_____

_____

_____

_____

_____

_____

_____

_____

_____

_____

_____

_____

_____

"God is in the midst of her, she will not be moved; God will help her when morning dawns." - Psalm 46:5

_____

_____

_____

_____

_____

_____

_____

_____

_____

_____

_____

_____

_____

_____

"God is in the midst of her, she will not be moved; God will help her when morning dawns." - Psalm 46:5

_____

_____

_____

_____

_____

_____

_____

_____

_____

_____

_____

_____

_____

_____

"God is in the midst of her, she will not be moved; God will help her when morning dawns." - Psalm 46:5

_____

_____

_____

_____

_____

_____

_____

_____

_____

_____

_____

_____

_____

_____

"God is in the midst of her, she will not be moved; God will help her when morning dawns." - Psalm 46:5

HERO**I**NE

nward

in·ward

/ ˈinwərd/

adverb

Existing within the mind, soul, or spirit, and often not expressed.

I know we just shared about the outward and logically, inward should have been first but then we would have misspelled heroine. However, regardless of how it is shared, your inward is just as important as your outward.

Not the pretend version but the real thing because your outward should be a reflection of your inward, without a disguise. The bible shares in Proverbs 15:13, "A glad heart makes a cheerful face, but by sorrow of heart the spirit is crushed."

Do you know the worst thing you can be, to the Kingdom of God, is a fake? Do you also know that faking it too long can cause you to forget what is real? Is that really worth jeopardizing your destiny?

"God is in the midst of her, she will not be moved; God will help her when morning dawns." - Psalm 46:5

Isn't constantly trying to cover up the fact your heart is broken, tiring? Does it not wear you out to consistently try to hide the messed up parts of your past instead of dealing with it? Are you not worn out from acting like you're okay?

Being dressed up on the outside but tore up on the inside is like putting a clean bag in an unclean garbage can. Although the bag is clean, when you remove it, the garbage can will still be dirty, funky and unclean. Or it's like trying to cover red with white, without properly priming; it'll bleed through every time.

Mend your inward because it will help your outward. Put right your inward because you owe yourself peace. Heal what you've been bandaging because the time of your restoration is at hand. Even if that means staging your own intervention to get clean. It's time, beloved, because the more you drag it out, the longer you will remain in bondage. You can be free but it begins with your willingness to start within.

Are you ready?

This is my prayer for you.

"I pray that God, the source of hope, will fill you completely with joy and peace because you trust in him. Then you will overflow with confident hope through the power of the Holy Spirit." - Romans 15:13

"God is in the midst of her, she will not be moved; God will help her when morning dawns." - Psalm 46:5

_____

_____

_____

_____

_____

_____

_____

_____

_____

_____

_____

_____

_____

_____

_____

_____

"God is in the midst of her, she will not be moved; God will help her when morning dawns." - Psalm 46:5

_____

_____

_____

_____

_____

_____

_____

_____

_____

_____

_____

_____

_____

_____

_____

"God is in the midst of her, she will not be moved; God will help her when morning dawns." - Psalm 46:5

"God is in the midst of her, she will not be moved; God will help her when morning dawns." - Psalm 46:5

"God is in the midst of her, she will not be moved; God will help her when morning dawns." - Psalm 46:5

_____

_____

_____

_____

_____

_____

_____

_____

_____

_____

_____

_____

_____

_____

_____

_____

"God is in the midst of her, she will not be moved; God will help her when morning dawns." - Psalm 46:5

_____

_____

_____

_____

_____

_____

_____

_____

_____

_____

_____

_____

_____

_____

_____

_____

"God is in the midst of her, she will not be moved; God will help her when morning dawns." - Psalm 46:5

_____

_____

_____

_____

_____

_____

_____

_____

_____

_____

_____

_____

_____

"God is in the midst of her, she will not be moved; God will help her when morning dawns." - Psalm 46:5

_____

_____

_____

_____

_____

_____

_____

_____

_____

_____

_____

_____

_____

_____

"God is in the midst of her, she will not be moved; God will help her when morning dawns." - Psalm 46:5

_____

_____

_____

_____

_____

_____

_____

_____

_____

_____

_____

_____

_____

_____

"God is in the midst of her, she will not be moved; God will help her when morning dawns." - Psalm 46:5

HEROI**N**E

𝒩otwithstanding

not·with·stand·ing

/ nätwiTH'standiNG, nätwiT̲H̲'standiNG/

preposition

> In spite of.

Notwithstanding what you've had to go through, you are still blessed. In spite of the obstacles placed on your path, you are still walking it. Aside from what you have had to endure, you still trust God.

Why? He made you strong enough to fight on. He made you to bounce back after the continued punches by the world. He made you to push on even when pain stopped you in your tracks. This is why you have no choice but to become addicted to the heroine you are. It doesn't make sense any other way.

Girl, you were made for this! Girl, you got this! Girl, this is yours! I know because when God created you, He did so with the strength to persevere and

"God is in the midst of her, she will not be moved; God will help her when morning dawns." - Psalm 46:5

overcome. All you have to do is change the way you talk.

Instead of saying I can't say, notwithstanding what man says about me, I am still worthy.

Instead of saying I am broke say, notwithstanding my finances, I shall not be without.

Instead of saying the darkness will overtake me, say notwithstanding my weeping, joy will come.

Instead of saying I am perishing in the fight say, notwithstanding my storms, I will live.

And instead of counting what you've lost or the many times you have been denied say, notwithstanding what I have to lose or what my natural eyes see, I will make it.

Make this your prayer ...

Dear God,

"I praise you, for I am fearfully and wonderfully made. Wonderful are your works; my soul knows it very well. My frame was not hidden from you, when I was being made in secret, intricately woven in the depths of the earth. Your eyes saw my unformed substance; in your book were written, every one of them, the days that were formed for me, when as yet there was none of them. How precious to me are your thoughts, O God! How vast is the sum of them! If I would count them, they are more than the sand. I awake, and I am still with you." Amen.

Psalm 139:13-18

"God is in the midst of her, she will not be moved; God will help her when morning dawns." - Psalm 46:5

_____

_____

_____

_____

_____

_____

_____

_____

_____

_____

_____

_____

_____

_____

_____

"God is in the midst of her, she will not be moved; God will help her when morning dawns." - Psalm 46:5

_____

_____

_____

_____

_____

_____

_____

_____

_____

_____

_____

_____

_____

_____

"God is in the midst of her, she will not be moved; God will help her when morning dawns." - Psalm 46:5

_____

_____

_____

_____

_____

_____

_____

_____

_____

_____

_____

_____

_____

_____

"God is in the midst of her, she will not be moved; God will help her when morning dawns." - Psalm 46:5

_____

_____

_____

_____

_____

_____

_____

_____

_____

_____

_____

_____

_____

_____

_____

_____

"God is in the midst of her, she will not be moved; God will help her when morning dawns." - Psalm 46:5

_____

_____

_____

_____

_____

_____

_____

_____

_____

_____

_____

_____

_____

_____

"God is in the midst of her, she will not be moved; God will help her when morning dawns." - Psalm 46:5

_____

_____

_____

_____

_____

_____

_____

_____

_____

_____

_____

_____

_____

_____

"God is in the midst of her, she will not be moved; God will help her when morning dawns." - Psalm 46:5

"God is in the midst of her, she will not be moved; God will help her when morning dawns." - Psalm 46:5

_____

_____

_____

_____

_____

_____

_____

_____

_____

_____

_____

_____

_____

_____

_____

_____

"God is in the midst of her, she will not be moved; God will help her when morning dawns." - Psalm 46:5

"God is in the midst of her, she will not be moved; God will help her when morning dawns." - Psalm 46:5

HEROINE

Effectual

ef·fec·tu·al

/ əˈfek(t)SH(oo͞)əl/

adjective

Successful in producing a desired or intended result; effective.

We have gone through almost every letter within the word HEROINE. We now know, we have to be habitable before we can embody and we get there by being refined which should change our outward and inward notwithstanding. But what does all this mean? What is the point?

Good questions, both of which can be answered.

The point of habitable, embody, refine, outward, inward and notwithstanding is to finally get you to the E. See, you cannot be a HEROINE without the E and the reason you have to go through all of the previous is in order for you to become effectual.

"God is in the midst of her, she will not be moved; God will help her when morning dawns." - Psalm 46:5

Effectual is being successful in producing a desired or intended result. In other words; effective.

Do you think any of these big companies, successful business owners and distinguished men and women of God are successful on their first attempts? No because there is a process you have to go through before you are effectual.

This is why you have to understand that you cannot be a HEROINE without every letter. Yes, I can remove the INE and call you a hero but without the 'E', you are not effective. And you cannot get to the E without going through the 'I' and the 'N'.

Don't rush the process. You become a HEROINE by being effectual in what you do. And this happens because you did not allow your fears or failures to stop you. You are a HEROINE because you did not allow man's denial to strip you of your purpose.

You are a HEROINE because you did not quit. You pushed. Through six letters, you pushed. Through the hardest process, you pushed and you've made it.

Don't count this a small victory because beloved, not everybody can rock the title of heroine but you can. Why? Because you have been effectual in what God has asked of you.

Claim your title of HEROINE ADDICT. Cry loud so that all can hear you say, "I am a HEROINE ADDICT, addicted to the greatness of God within me."

"Girl, what are you addicted to?"

"The HEROINE that I am."

A HEROINE by definition is a woman who, in the opinion of others, has special achievements, abilities or personal qualities and is regarded as a role model.

Is that you? Of course it is.

Dear God,

Although there are times I question you, thank you for the process. Even during the times I want to give in, thank you for the process. Thank you for the closed doors, the many failed attempts and the times I had to fall because they made me effective to now call myself the heroine that I am. Amen.

"God is in the midst of her, she will not be moved; God will help her when morning dawns." - Psalm 46:5

_____

_____

_____

_____

_____

_____

_____

_____

_____

_____

_____

_____

_____

_____

"God is in the midst of her, she will not be moved; God will help her when morning dawns." - Psalm 46:5

false

_____

_____

_____

_____

_____

_____

_____

_____

_____

_____

_____

_____

_____

_____

"God is in the midst of her, she will not be moved; God will help her when morning dawns." - Psalm 46:5

_____

_____

_____

_____

_____

_____

_____

_____

_____

_____

_____

_____

_____

_____

"God is in the midst of her, she will not be moved; God will help her when morning dawns." - Psalm 46:5

_____

_____

_____

_____

_____

_____

_____

_____

_____

_____

_____

_____

_____

_____

_____

_____

"God is in the midst of her, she will not be moved; God will help her when morning dawns." - Psalm 46:5

_____

_____

_____

_____

_____

_____

_____

_____

_____

_____

_____

_____

_____

_____

"God is in the midst of her, she will not be moved; God will help her when morning dawns." - Psalm 46:5

_____

_____

_____

_____

_____

_____

_____

_____

_____

_____

_____

_____

_____

_____

"God is in the midst of her, she will not be moved; God will help her when morning dawns." - Psalm 46:5

_____

_____

_____

_____

_____

_____

_____

_____

_____

_____

_____

_____

_____

_____

"God is in the midst of her, she will not be moved; God will help her when morning dawns." - Psalm 46:5

_____

_____

_____

_____

_____

_____

_____

_____

_____

_____

_____

_____

_____

_____

_____

_____

"God is in the midst of her, she will not be moved; God will help her when morning dawns." - Psalm 46:5

_____

_____

_____

_____

_____

_____

_____

_____

_____

_____

_____

_____

_____

"God is in the midst of her, she will not be moved; God will help her when morning dawns." - Psalm 46:5

_____

_____

_____

_____

_____

_____

_____

_____

_____

_____

_____

_____

_____

_____

_____

"God is in the midst of her, she will not be moved; God will help her when morning dawns." - Psalm 46:5

_____

_____

_____

_____

_____

_____

_____

_____

_____

_____

_____

_____

_____

_____

"God is in the midst of her, she will not be moved; God will help her when morning dawns." - Psalm 46:5

_____

_____

_____

_____

_____

_____

_____

_____

_____

_____

_____

_____

_____

_____

_____

"God is in the midst of her, she will not be moved; God will help her when morning dawns." - Psalm 46:5

_____

_____

_____

_____

_____

_____

_____

_____

_____

_____

_____

_____

_____

_____

"God is in the midst of her, she will not be moved; God will help her when morning dawns." - Psalm 46:5

_____

_____

_____

_____

_____

_____

_____

_____

_____

_____

_____

_____

_____

_____

"God is in the midst of her, she will not be moved; God will help her when morning dawns." - Psalm 46:5

_____

_____

_____

_____

_____

_____

_____

_____

_____

_____

_____

_____

_____

_____

_____

"God is in the midst of her, she will not be moved; God will help her when morning dawns." - Psalm 46:5

_____

_____

_____

_____

_____

_____

_____

_____

_____

_____

_____

_____

_____

_____

_____

"God is in the midst of her, she will not be moved; God will help her when morning dawns." - Psalm 46:5

_____

_____

_____

_____

_____

_____

_____

_____

_____

_____

_____

_____

_____

"God is in the midst of her, she will not be moved; God will help her when morning dawns." - Psalm 46:5

"God is in the midst of her, she will not be moved; God will help her when morning dawns." - Psalm 46:5

_____

_____

_____

_____

_____

_____

_____

_____

_____

_____

_____

_____

_____

_____

_____

_____

"God is in the midst of her, she will not be moved; God will help her when morning dawns." - Psalm 46:5

_____

_____

_____

_____

_____

_____

_____

_____

_____

_____

_____

_____

_____

_____

"God is in the midst of her, she will not be moved; God will help her when morning dawns." - Psalm 46:5

"God is in the midst of her, she will not be moved; God will help her when morning dawns." - Psalm 46:5

_____

_____

_____

_____

_____

_____

_____

_____

_____

_____

_____

_____

_____

_____

_____

_____

"God is in the midst of her, she will not be moved; God will help her when morning dawns." - Psalm 46:5

_____

_____

_____

_____

_____

_____

_____

_____

_____

_____

_____

_____

_____

_____

"God is in the midst of her, she will not be moved; God will help her when morning dawns." - Psalm 46:5

_____

_____

_____

_____

_____

_____

_____

_____

_____

_____

_____

_____

_____

_____

"God is in the midst of her, she will not be moved; God will help her when morning dawns." - Psalm 46:5

_____

_____

_____

_____

_____

_____

_____

_____

_____

_____

_____

_____

_____

_____

"God is in the midst of her, she will not be moved; God will help her when morning dawns." - Psalm 46:5

_____

_____

_____

_____

_____

_____

_____

_____

_____

_____

_____

_____

_____

_____

"God is in the midst of her, she will not be moved; God will help her when morning dawns." - Psalm 46:5

_____

_____

_____

_____

_____

_____

_____

_____

_____

_____

_____

_____

_____

_____

"God is in the midst of her, she will not be moved; God will help her when morning dawns." - Psalm 46:5

_____

_____

_____

_____

_____

_____

_____

_____

_____

_____

_____

_____

_____

_____

"God is in the midst of her, she will not be moved; God will help her when morning dawns." - Psalm 46:5

_____

_____

_____

_____

_____

_____

_____

_____

_____

_____

_____

_____

_____

_____

"God is in the midst of her, she will not be moved; God will help her when morning dawns." - Psalm 46:5

_____

_____

_____

_____

_____

_____

_____

_____

_____

_____

_____

_____

_____

_____

_____

"God is in the midst of her, she will not be moved; God will help her when morning dawns." - Psalm 46:5

_____

_____

_____

_____

_____

_____

_____

_____

_____

_____

_____

_____

_____

_____

_____

_____

"God is in the midst of her, she will not be moved; God will help her when morning dawns." - Psalm 46:5

_____

_____

_____

_____

_____

_____

_____

_____

_____

_____

_____

_____

_____

_____

"God is in the midst of her, she will not be moved; God will help her when morning dawns." - Psalm 46:5

_____

_____

_____

_____

_____

_____

_____

_____

_____

_____

_____

_____

_____

_____

"God is in the midst of her, she will not be moved; God will help her when morning dawns." - Psalm 46:5

_____

_____

_____

_____

_____

_____

_____

_____

_____

_____

_____

_____

_____

_____

_____

"God is in the midst of her, she will not be moved; God will help her when morning dawns." - Psalm 46:5

_____

_____

_____

_____

_____

_____

_____

_____

_____

_____

_____

_____

_____

"God is in the midst of her, she will not be moved; God will help her when morning dawns." - Psalm 46:5

_____

_____

_____

_____

_____

_____

_____

_____

_____

_____

_____

_____

_____

_____

"God is in the midst of her, she will not be moved; God will help her when morning dawns." - Psalm 46:5

_____

_____

_____

_____

_____

_____

_____

_____

_____

_____

_____

_____

_____

_____

"God is in the midst of her, she will not be moved; God will help her when morning dawns." - Psalm 46:5

_____

_____

_____

_____

_____

_____

_____

_____

_____

_____

_____

_____

_____

_____

_____

"God is in the midst of her, she will not be moved; God will help her when morning dawns." - Psalm 46:5

_____

_____

_____

_____

_____

_____

_____

_____

_____

_____

_____

_____

_____

_____

"God is in the midst of her, she will not be moved; God will help her when morning dawns." - Psalm 46:5

_____

_____

_____

_____

_____

_____

_____

_____

_____

_____

_____

_____

_____

_____

_____

"God is in the midst of her, she will not be moved; God will help her when morning dawns." - Psalm 46:5

_____

_____

_____

_____

_____

_____

_____

_____

_____

_____

_____

_____

_____

_____

"God is in the midst of her, she will not be moved; God will help her when morning dawns." - Psalm 46:5

Journal to Destiny

HONORABLE! | ESTABLISHED
RIGHTEOUS | OBEDIENT
INCORRUPTIBLE | NOBLE
EDIFYING

HEROINE ... That's you!

"God is in the midst of her, she will not be moved; God will help her when morning dawns." - Psalm 46:5

About the author

 *Lakisha Johnson, native Memphian and author of ten titles was born to write. She'll tell you that "Writing didn't find me, it's was engraved within me during my creation." Along with being an author, she is an ordained minister, co-pastor, wife, mother and the product of a large family. She is an avid blogger at kishasdailydevotional.com and social media poster where she utilizes her gifts to encourage others to tap into their God given talents. She won't claim to be the best at what she does nor does she have all the answers, she is simply grateful to be used by God.*

You can find her on:

Facebook: KishaDJohnson | AuthorLakisha | Twins Write 2

Twitter: @ _kishajohnson | Instagram: kishajohnson

Snapchat: Authorlakisha | Email: authorlakisha@gmail.com

Amazon by searching Lakisha Johnson

"God is in the midst of her, she will not be moved; God will help her when morning dawns." - Psalm 46:5